Summ
of

On Tyranny
Timothy Snyder

Conversation Starters

By BookHabits

Please Note: This is an unofficial Conversation Starters guide. If you have not yet read the original work, you can <u>purchase the original book here.</u>

We hope you enjoy this complementary guide from BookHabits. Our mission is to aid readers and reading groups with quality, thought provoking material to in the discovery and discussions on some of today's favorite books.

Bonus Downloads

*Get Free Books with **Any Purchase** of Conversation Starters!*

Every purchase comes with a FREE download!

Add spice to any conversation
Never run out of things to say
Spend time with those you love

Get it Now

or Click Here.

Scan Your Phone

Tips for Using Conversation Starters:

EVERY GOOD BOOK CONTAINS A WORLD FAR DEEPER THAN the surface of its pages. Questions herein are designed to bring us beneath the surface of the page and invite us into the world that lives on. These questions can be used to:

- Foster a deeper understanding of the book
- Promote an atmosphere of discussion for groups
- Assist in the study of the book, either individually or corporately
- Explore unseen realms of the book as never seen before

Table of Contents

Introducing *On Tyranny*

"On Tyranny: Twenty Lessons from the Twentieth Century" is Timothy Snyder's how to guide on how to resist tyranny in our day and age by walking his reader through 20 lessons, enriched with examples and case studies found throughout history for each of his points. Throughout his book, Snyder is trying to persuade his reader to prepare and anticipate to resist tyranny in our day. Specifically, in the realm of the American political system. He seeks to arm his audience with the necessities they must acquire in order to resist oppression from Donald Trump's administration and their rule over the United States. A scholar of European history that has surrounded fascism, Snyder argues against the idea that Americans have been and always will be immune to the calamities of politics and wars that Europe has faced throughout its history. "On Tyranny" brings to light the very real patterns of fascist Europe that can be seen in modern day America. Even with its systems of checks and balances, Snyder argues that the country is in the same grave danger as those who suffered through the Nazi regime. He argues that we simply cannot sit idly by and watch democracy fly out of the window. He demands action and persistence by any and all American citizens to defend their democracy and not give into the tyranny that they face. He argues that history should not "run its course," so to speak, but we must press on with earnestness in creating the future where democracy remains and thrives.

At the core of Snyder's twenty lessons is the fact that American citizens should not give in to their leaders. He discusses how those who found themselves under Hitler's rule did so voluntarily, without a fight. According to him, authoritarianism only comes into play when it is freely given. Snyder discusses how Hitler's regime was only able to thrive because of leaders who were afraid to lose their jobs and citizens who voluntarily handed over their obedience to the regime's goals. Snyder also cites the rise of Communism and the depletion of democracy in 1946 Czechoslovakia, where the Communist Party won the popular vote—a form of voluntary obedience.

One of Snyder's particular poignant lessons lies in the second lesson. It is in this lesson that he challenges his reader to "defend institutions." He exhorts American citizens to uphold courts, the press, trade unions, and the like. His argument here is that ensuring the strength of institutions that surround the executive office of the country will ensure that that office stays in check—that tyranny will not overcome every other facet of the society in which Americans live. He argues that we must uphold these institutions because they simply cannot uphold themselves. We depend on them just as they depend on us. Therefore, we as U.S. citizens must play our part in that relationship.

Etched throughout many of Snyder's lessons is the lesson in which he calls for American citizens to "take responsibility for the face of the world." In essence, this lesson challenges Americans to be aware of and alert to the signs of political propaganda. He wants his readers to understand and recognize words or schemes that should worry us, including but not limited to phrases like "fake news" and things that fall under the jurisdiction of "alternate facts." He wants Americans to come at politics with a persistently skeptical lens, looking for what might be the underlining message or purpose to the choices made within the political world. Snyder looks at how well-versed Hitler and the Nazis were in the ways of persuasive language. It was not their guns that got them in power, but the words they were so good at constructing into a language comfortable and swaying to the minds of their listeners. He wants Americans to dig deeper into exactly what "truth" is and where it can be found—to not rely on their country's leaders to give it to them, but to rely on themselves to find it wherever and however they can.

The bold "so what?" of Snyder's work here is that tyranny can be survived and overcome, and even prevented if we stay strong in our conviction to do so. He wants Americans to remain calm when all seems to be going wrong and to establish and maintain a life that is private. Throughout his book, he calls on the events of history to help us understand how we can be courageous in this trying time in the history of the world. To him, tyranny does not have to be the end result.

Discussion Questions

"Get Ready to Enter a New World"

Tip: Begin with questions dealing with broader issues to ensure ample time for quality discussions. Read through all discussion questions before engaging.

~~~

question 1

Snyder often cites Nazi Germany as an example of what the United States could become if tyranny is not kept in check. Do you see any flaws in this example when compared to the U.S.?

~~~

~~~

question 2

Snyder argues that institutions cannot uphold
themselves; he says we must uphold them. Do you
agree?

~~~

~~~

question 3

Snyder offers up a solution of being hyper aware of the language used by politicians to detect propaganda. Do you think such a simple solution will help change the course of history?

~~~

~~~

question 4

Snyder challenges Americans to dig deeper into finding truth. With so many "alternative facts," do you think this is possible?

~~~

~~~

question 5

Snyder claims that Hitler's regime started when people gave their obedience voluntarily to the regime. Do you think this is a fair argument?

~~~

~~~

question 6

The 1930s was a time of hardship and poverty. Snyder argues that the leaders of the Nazi regime stayed in their jobs out of fear. Is it possible they stayed out of a fear of poverty and not so much of the regime?

~~~

~~~

question 7

Snyder claims Americans have a sense of being immune to the political calamities like those Europe has faced in the past. Do you think Americans actually think this?

~~~

~~~

question 8

Snyder discusses that Communism came to be
after people voted for the party, demolishing the
role of democracy voluntarily. Would you argue
that they did so out of fear of the already violent
party's actions?

~~~

~~~

question 9

Snyder argues that we must keep institutions in check to keep tyranny at bay. Do you agree that surrounding institutions can keep the presidential administration in check?

~~~

~~~

question 10

Snyder offers that we should look at politics through a skeptical lens. Do you think that's a fair suggestion? Do you think that it's healthy to do so?

~~~

~~~

question 11

Snyder says that the checks and balances of democracy are no longer enough to avoid tyranny. Do you agree with this statement?

~~~

~~~

question 12

According to Snyder, tyranny came to power because of the persuasive language those leaders used. Would you agree with this statement? Why or why not?

~~~

~~~

question 13

Snyder argues that we each uphold our own private lives, including those of political leaders. Do you think this is a fair argument?

~~~

~~~

question 14

Snyder discusses how a world of "alternative facts" leads to fascism because everyone is looking out for themselves instead of looking out for the truth. Is this a fair argument?

~~~

~~~

question 15

Snyder talks about how creating "fake news" alters the view of the public to one side, promoting a non-democracy society. Would you agree with this argument?

~~~

~~~

question 16

"On Tyranny" gained a spot of number three on the New York Time's Bestseller List. Why do you think it gained such praise?

~~~

~~~

question 17

"On Tyranny" is pocket sized and is a very short read. Do you think its similarities to traditional manifestos is coincidental or purposeful?

~~~

~~~

question 18

Snyder claims to have written mostly for young
Americans that need to be more aware of the state
of their country. Does "On Tyranny" read this way
or would you say it's a book for all Americans?

~~~

~~~

question 19

"On Tyranny" gained 4.5 stars from Amazon. Why do you think people are fascinated with the topic?

~~~

~~~

question 20

"On Tyranny" seeks to inspire American citizens to fight against and prevent tyranny. Would you say it accomplishes this goal effectively?

~~~

Introducing the Author

Timothy Snyder was born in August of 1969 in the southwest region of Ohio to Christine Hadley and Estel Eugene Snyder. His mother, Christine, was a stay at home mom and his father, Estel, was a veterinarian by profession. Snyder attended Centerville High School in Centerville Ohio. He went on to gain his bachelor's degree in history and political science from Brown University. After gaining this undergraduate degree, Snyder went on to gain his Doctorate of Philosophy from the University of Oxford in modern history. He finished at Oxford in 1997 and was a Marshall Scholar at Balliol College at Oxford from 1991 to 1994.

Snyder has had quite a career in the academic field. From 1994 to 1995, he gained fellowships from Centre national de la recherche scientifique in Paris, the Institut für die Wissenschaften vom Menschen in Vienna in 1996, Harvard University's Olin Institute for Strategic Studies in 1997, and he gained the role of Academic Scholar at Harvard University's Weatherhead Center for International Affairs from 1998 to 2001.

His professional career is just as impressive as his academic one. He has held several positions at universities and organizations, including instructor at the College of Europe Warsaw

Campus, Baron Velge Chair at the Université libre de Bruxelles, Cleveringa Chair at the University of Leiden, Philippe Romain Chair at the London School of Economics, and Stanford University's René Girard Lecturer in 2013. He was Yale University's Bird White Housum Professor of History and then went on to gain the Richard C. Levin Professorship of History.

Snyder can speak, write, and read several languages. Among these are French, Polish, Czech, Slovak, Russian, and Belarusian. He holds a place as a member of the Committee of Conscience within the United States Holocaust Memorial Museum in Washington, DC.

Snyder has published several works, including historical books. Among which are "Bloodlands: Europe Between Hitler and Stalin," "Black Earth: The Holocaust as History and Warning," and "The Road to Unfreedom: Russia, Europe, America." His work explores not only history, but the making of history in the present day and how the two coincide and affect one another.

Snyder is currently a professor at Yale University, where he teaches a two-part lecture course in which he teaches the history of Eastern Europe, pre- and post-1914. He previously talk a seminar at Yale University, covering communism in Eastern Europe.

Snyder has spoken out on several occasions concerning the Trump administration. When asked if he would compare Trump to Hitler, Snyder will underhandedly take control over the entire government just as Hitler did and democracy will be subverted in the United States. He states that the comparison of patterns between Hitler and Trump's administration are far too similar to be ignored. He claims that American citizens should prepare themselves to resist whatever may come so that history cannot and will not repeat itself.

Snyder is married to another Yale University professor, Marci Shore. She teaches European cultural and intellectual history. They were married in 2005 and have two children together.

Bonus Downloads

Get Free Books with __Any Purchase__ of Conversation Starters!

Every purchase comes with a FREE download!

Add spice to any conversation
Never run out of things to say
Spend time with those you love

Scan Your Phone

Fireside Questions

"What would you do?"

Tip: These questions can be a fun exercise as it spurs creativity among the readers by allowing alternate scene endings and "if this was you" questions.

~~~

question 21

Snyder can read, speak, and write in several languages. How do you think this has affected his study of history?

~~~

~~~

question 22

Snyder has been a part of the academic world in several countries. How do you think this has affected his research for "On Tyranny"?

~~~

~~~

question 23

Snyder has written books in the past about historical events and how they affect the present day. How does "On Tyranny" fit into that motif? Does it?

~~~

question 24

Snyder is very antagonistic toward the Trump administration. Would you say this is a healthy view when writing about defending democracy in "On Tyranny"?

~~~

~~~

question 25

Snyder gained his undergraduate degree in both history and political science. How does this effect his arguments in "On Tyranny"?

~~~

~~~

question 26

Snyder is quick to point out the similarities between Hitler and the current administration in America. What other regimes/political models would you compare the U.S. to?

~~~

~~~

question 27

Snyder is a professor of European history. If you were in his field, would you also write about American politics?

~~~

~~~

question 28

Snyder remains an American citizen even when he fears the tyranny America is facing. Would you change your citizenship if you had the same historical knowledge he has about tyranny?

~~~

~ ~ ~

question 29

Snyder cites persuasive language as a cause for the Nazi regime. Would you use your persuasive language instead to defend and uphold democracy?

~ ~ ~

~~~

question 30

Snyder states that we must uphold our private lives, including those of political leaders. Would you respect the private lives of political leaders if you were a journalist?

~~~

Quiz Questions

"Ready to Announce the Winners?"

Tip: Create a leaderboard and track scores to see who gets the most correct answers. Winners required. Prizes optional.

~~~

quiz question 1

True or False: Snyder compares the current political administration in America to Nazi Germany.

~~~

~~~

quiz question 2

Snyder writes lessons in his book about how to fight against and prevent tyranny. There are ____ lessons throughout "On Tyranny."

~~~

~~~

quiz question 3

True or False: Snyder uses Eastern European history to cite examples of tyranny.

~~~

~~~

quiz question 4

True or False: Snyder claims that "alternative facts" are good.

~~~

~~~

quiz question 5

True or False: Snyder thinks that institutions can thrive on their own without the support of American citizens.

~~~

~ ~ ~

quiz question 6

True or False: Snyder thinks Americans are right
to think that they are immune to fascism.

~ ~ ~

~~~

quiz question 7

True or False: Snyder wants history to run its course without interference from anyone.

~~~

quiz question 8

True or False: Snyder grew up in Ohio.

~~~

quiz question 9

True or False: Snyder's mom was a lawyer.

~~~

~ ~ ~

quiz question 10

True or False: Snyder has taught at only one Ivy league school.

~ ~ ~

~~~

quiz question 11

True or False: Snyder has taught at universities and institutions around the world.

~~~

quiz question 12

True or False: Snyder knows only English.

Quiz Answers

1. True
2. 20
3. True
4. False
5. False
6. False
7. False
8. True
9. False
10. False
11. True
12. False

Ways to Continue Your Reading

EVERY month, our team runs through a wide selection of books to pick the best titles for readers and reading groups, and promotes these titles to our thousands of readers – sometimes with free downloads, sale dates, and additional brochures.

Click here to sign up for these benefits.

If you have not yet read the original work or would like to read it again, you can purchase the original book here.

Bonus Downloads

*Get Free Books with **Any Purchase** of Conversation Starters!*

Every purchase comes with a FREE download!

Add spice to any conversation
Never run out of things to say
Spend time with those you love

Get it Now

or Click Here.

Scan Your Phone

On the Next Page...

If you found this book helpful to your discussions and rate it a 4 or 5, please write us a review on the next page.

Any length would be fine but we'd appreciate hearing you more! We'd be very encouraged.

Till next time,

BookHabits

"Loving Books is Actually a Habit"

Made in the USA
Middletown, DE
28 September 2019